ROSEMARY FOLKS

Souls'

Confession

BY
Rosemary Folks

SOUL'S CONFESSION

All rights reserved. No parts of this book may be used or reproduced in any matter whatsoever without written permission from the Publisher, except in the case of brief citations embodied in critical articles and reviews. Any members of educational institutions wishing to photocopy part or all the work for classroom use, or publishers who would like to obtain permission to include the work in an anthology, should send inquiries to the Author/ Publisher

Copyright©2017 Rosemary Folks
ALL RIGHT RESERVED
ISBN:978-0-692-99373-6

ROSEMARY FOLKS

Thank you for purchasing Soul's Confession.

I dedicate this book first and fore-most to the God of this Universe, The Great I Am and to my Lord and Savior Jesus. I finally completed this book because of their Love, Grace and Mercy.

Secondly, I dedicate this book to my family and friends. Thank you all for your love and support. Thanks to my Mom Annie Folks and my Dad Lucius Folks.

Lastly, To my Dearest friend Sonia Robles. Thank You for being there for me throughout my many trails. Love You.

Remember that the Creator of all Existence is in Love with you, Yes You.

Special Thank You to the Holy Spirit for helping me complete this book.

SOUL'S CONFESSION

CONTENT

Acknowledgment

Poems

Season One

Abortion   1
Acquainted with Gloom   2
African American   3-5
Alone, where do I Fit in?   6
Before and Now   7
Burning Questions   8
Come Upon Me   9
Confused   10
Conquer with Truth   11
Conscious Dream   12
Crack Head   13, 14
Cries of Black Teenage Boys   15-17
Don't Worry   18, 19
Flight 800 Unforgettable Lost'   20
Homeless Person   21, 22
How Can I   23
I am Here not to Raise a Man   24, 25
James Baldwin   26, 27
Melancholy   28
Music of Miles   29, 30
Once Again   31, 32
Poetry from Within   33

ROSEMARY FOLKS

Prostitute   34
Questionable Farewell   35
Realization   36, 37
Response to Cries of Black Teenage Boys   38, 39
Rooms   40
Silent Rage   41
Slave Girl   42
Solid Foundation   43
Sugar Daddy   44
Suicide Reflection and Still I Breathe   45, 46
The Devil Never Shines in the Light   47, 48
The Last Laugh is Mines   49
They did not Win   50, 51
Voices of the Mind   52, 53
We   54
When   55

Season Two

Abrupt Sensuality   59
Are you the one   60, 61
But 62
Embracing thoughts   63
Emotions Concealed   64
First Encounter   65
God has Hugged you   66
Hey Daddy it is I   67
I am in your Hands   68, 69
I Still Love you   70, 71

SOUL'S CONFESSION

I Want to Live   72, 73
Inner Talk   74
Jesus Speaks   75, 76
Knowingly   77
Matthew 6:30, 33   78, 79
More of you Less of Me   80, 81
My Love   82
Oneness with my Child   83, 84
Praise   85
Realization   85
Souls' Confession   86, 87
Spirit is Awake   88
The Silent Whisper   89, 90
There is only one way to the Father   91-95
Thinking to my Heavenly Father   96
Thoughts to You   97, 98
Unforeseen Labor   99
You are in me   100
You See me with You Heart 101, 102
Your Groove Moves Me   103, 104

ROSEMARY FOLKS

Acknowledgment

My beliefs in and how I praise God may differ from yours, but I hope that we could look beyond the surface of human frailties and allow Love to govern our interactions. The more you spend time with Yahweh in his Words by meditating on them, you will engage in an intimate relationship with Him. If you believe that Jesus died for the sins of Man and He is your Lord and Saviour, I am to call you sister or brother. REMINDER: 1 Corinthians 1:10, "Now I beseech You, Brethren, by the name of Our Lord Jesus Christ, that ye all speak the same thing, and that there be no division among you; but that ye be perfectly joined together in the same mind and in the same judgment." We as Yah children must keep focused on the foundation of our Truth and refuse Satan antics of division. We all have gifts and talents that would encourage others to live for truth, justice, and righteousness. And, the Gift of Poetry is mines. Ever since Yahushua (Jesus) ascended back to Heaven; from that day until his return, we are living in the Last Days. So, I encourage you to spend time with our Heavenly Father the Great I Am and his son Jesus while you are still breathing in this shell of a body. Satan knows he only has a minute left on this Earth. He will do all he can to mislead as many as he could because that is his

SOUL'S CONFESSION

purpose. He is an imitator of Light. He knows that Heaven is real, and he does not have a chance in Hell of ever returning. Our purposes as true followers of Jesus are to remind people of why He came and who He is. A few reasons why Jesus came to Earth the first time. 1. To reveal the Father. (Matthew **11:7)** 2. To be a ransom for many. (Matthew 20:28) 3. To save Mankind. (John 3:17, Luke 19:10) 4. To Preach the Good News of the Kingdom of the Great I Am (Luke 4:43) 5. To bring division. (Luke 12:51) 6. To do the Will of the Father. (John 6:38) 7. To give the Father's words. (John 17:8) 8. To die and to destroy Satan's power. (Hebrew 2:14) 9. To give life. (John 10:10, 28) and 10. To taste death for everyone. (Hebrew 2:9). When Yahushua came to Earth the first time, he came through a womb of a Virgin Woman, Mary. His Second Coming would be him descending from the cloud. (Luke21:27)

ROSEMARY FOLKS

A few reasons for His Second Coming. 1. A priceless inheritance for all believers. (1 Peter 1:3-5) 2. For believers to be like Him. (1 John 3:2) 3. To destroy all ungodly people. (2 Peter 3:7) 4. To bring everything under authority. (Ephesians 1:10) 5. For believers to be reconciled to the Father. (Colossians 1:20) 6. To change the believers physical body. (Philippians 3:21) and 7. For believers to live forever with the Great I Am. (1 John 2:17). Jesus is our Lord and Saviour; He became God in the Flesh. Right now, at this very moment, He is seated at the right Hand of the Great I Am (Matthew 26:64), waiting for the Father's command. I serve a God that is Alive. We must tell people about the gift of Salvation.

ROSEMARY FOLKS

Abortion

Who gave your life?
Your Mother, your father, The Holy Spirit
Why in the world should you take a life?
Now You will never know
what that child Would have become.
That child could have made you smile
When you were down and out
Now you have nightmares
That child would have heard you scream and shout
This poem is not to make you remember all
The unnecessary and uncanny pain
You put yourself through
Next time you hear your inner conscious say, "You are Pregnant."
Remember that that child is not you.

SOUL'S CONFESSION

Acquainted with Gloom

My Heaven and hell is present
As I shut down emotions
Feelings of truth is nowhere to be found
I have turned life's thoughts into living nightmares
I am unable to distinguish
From what is real from what is not
Long ago I have learnt to disconnect from self
That was the only way I felt free
My Spirit is going into an inferno
While my flesh is shivering to find comfort
I am willing to give all of me to anyone who say,
"I Need You"
They do not have to show affection back
But just knowing that I am what they need
Helps feed my fearful existence.

ROSEMARY FOLKS

African American

I have been asked, "Where are you from? Queens,
Brooklyn, the Bronx, Manhattan. I say that I am from
Africa
People focus on my appearance and say stop playing
I am not playing,
Even though I have not been there physically
But I have been to Africa plenty of times emotionally and mentally
Every time elderly women of European descendant stare at me
and clenches their pocket book
as I sit beside them on a public bus station bench
Or in a Subway cart
makes me realize that they are still afraid of my freedom.
If I choose to wear baggy pants, my hair in breads bamboo
earrings, and a three quarter Black leather jacket
Just to allow myself to be recognized as a product of my environment
Am I asking for their fear?
The way my fore-fathers sent signals through drums, sung
songs of freedom, and gathered together for fellowship
Did they ask for their fear?
Now, if I wear a nice two-piece satin,

SOUL'S CONFESSION

red, black, and green skirt suit
with a scarf, hat, and shoes to match
They will stare and smile
And, that says to me that they approve
as if I needed their approval.
The way my fore-mothers breast fed their new born
cleaned their houses and ran around butt naked
Their stare and smile suggest that they approved.
It does not matter how educated I am
or where I may have been or where I
may go to them
I am still a slave from Africa.
Even my mother is stuck on the notion
That since my great grandmother mother's mother was an
Irish Man
And that she was a Cherokee Indian
I should stop telling people that I am from Africa
I told her that I must accept where Man came from
So, I can pave the way for others
 Whomever consider themselves as
An African American
Should start living as such
Allow one to remember all the unbearable pain
Our ancestor endured just for us to be seen and heard
We went from being called People of Color to Colored,
Colored to Negro; Negro to Nigga, Nigga to Black, Black
to what we have been told to call ourselves today

ROSEMARY FOLKS

An African American
We accepted this name
We are worth more than that cotton we plucked
and worth more than that gold we dug up
with our bare hands
God does love us
Always remember,

>WE HAVE ALWAYS BEEN
>AN AFRICAN
>THEN
>AN AMERICAN.

SOUL'S CONFESSION

Alone, Where Do I Fit In

I have seen people pain and hurt
I wonder if they have seen mine
    Sometimes I ask myself "Where do I fit in?"
When someone asks me, "What should I do?"
I respond, "Do what is in your heart."
They seem to not comprehend
and ask me, "What do you mean?"
    Sometimes I ask myself "Where do I fit in?"
People see my smile
It is really upside down
But do they ask, "How are you, really?"
No, they don't
They are only seeing my physical being
    Sometimes I ask myself "Where do I fit in?"
I do not know who I should let in
or where I belong
I am sick and tired of singing this sad song
    Sometimes I ask myself "Where do I fit in?"
I know a love I wish to grab
But is it in this life time
She, I should choose to have
    Sometimes I ask myself "Where do I fit in?"
Right Now, I Feel I Have No One
Because I feel
    Alone, Where Do I Fit In?

ROSEMARY FOLKS

Before and Now

I look in the mirror and see the color that I am
My Ancestors have fought for my life to begin
the struggle they have been
Makes me feel that I too can survive Because
Harriett Tubman and Rosa Parks
Have never took a dive Educating myself,
"You are acting White." My peers say to me
They have chosen to close their eyes
They have refuse to see
That there is so much more to life
Than what our parents have taught us,
but we must believe in Jesus In Him we must trust.

SOUL'S CONFESSION

Burning Questions

Who is the hero in your life?
Is it the dead, the dying, or the living?
Why is that?
Do you know?
Are you being the best you can be?
Or do you feel that when you die, you will finally be?
Who are you there for?
Can they tell another that you they love?
If or when you kneel and pray
Who do you pray for, the dead, the dying, or the living?

ROSEMARY FOLKS

Come Upon Me

I intoxicate people
With my presence
They try to see through me
and find my treasures I have not yet spoken
but they think they know
My secrets and hopes.
I terrify them
With my silence
and they still hunger
for an understanding of me.
I can receive
And returning love
But not to anyone Whom chooses to judge I
Because of my outer beauty.

Confused

Mommy, where was you
When I needed you?
Poppa it was wrong to leave
After all the pain momma been through
Did someone hurt your heart other than my momma?
Is that the reason you felt you had to leave my sister, my brothers, and me? I have been on my hands in knees
Asking for either of you to hold me
but neither of you have
Now I think if I am mistreated by a Man
That is the way it should be.
Momma would come home from a party
And say to me
"Baby, Momma had an enjoyable time."
You would go into a rage and ask her "How did she spend her last dime?"
Now I am old enough
to become a parent of my own
I hope I would not be like neither of you
I just turned 13
And I think I am grown.

ROSEMARY FOLKS

Conquer with Truth

The rambling was going on in my head
Times like this I wish I was dead
I just want the chatter to stop
I continued to walk even though it would not
with all the beauty around me
I tried to focus on an object I can visually see
but the negative words to self just would not let me be
I took deep breathes in and out
Secretly, I wanted to shout
But I heard my inner voice say, "over, you can start this day." I stood at a corner
And closed my eyes
And forcefully told the bad memories goodbye
I was led to a J & R music store
Unaware that my God wanted to speak to me
No longer than ten minutes I have purchased a Lenny Kravitz tape
Who knew that the song Rosemary would strengthen my faith?
Moments like that lets me know
That the Great I Am cares
He is always near.

Conscious Dream

I just got my own place
The first thing I am doing is taking a bubble bath
in my own tub.
After, I will leave my own bathroom
I will go into My own bedroom
And allow my body
To air dry.
Then, I will go on Top of my own dresser
and take the powder,
Deodorant, lotion, and Body spray down
and will sit on
My own king size bed
And apply all the Hygienic Cosmetics to my body.
Girl, get up
I am about to go to work
You know I do not
Leave anyone in my house when I gone.

ROSEMARY FOLKS

Crack Head

"Let me go." I have screamed to the pipe
Still I caress it with all my might I run all night
Just to stop my conscious flight My get high partner Is now
clean and sober Now everyone wants to grab and hold her
I am not playing hating or nothing
I am just thinking back And Damn, were we something
Now, if I ask her to spot me a five or maybe a ten
She will say no, with this silly behind grin She is still my
peeps and all
And she will buy me a Meal and **it
But she knows damn well I need a fix
Now when I see her, she always tells me to take it one day
at a time   I joke around and
say, "that show used to come channel five."
As we depart, I secretly say, "She will hit the pipe again one
day."
I make sure that my child has what it needs
Before I give in and feed my Fein
One day my nine-year-old
Left a piece of paper on my bed
That read
The Meaning of Crack Head

SOUL'S CONFESSION

Crack

Remains

A

Conscious

Killer

Helping

Evil

Approach

Death.

ROSEMARY FOLKS

Cries of Black teenage boys

I didn't realize I potted trained a thug
No more hugs
He traded them in for slugs
You see the streets taught him how to pack the heat
He did time in his mind Before he sat in a jail cell
With fire blurring through his vision It wasn't hard to tell
That sooner or later He will get trapped in the game
I wonder does he know That I love him the same
I don't condone what he did, it was wrong
But I write him long letters Telling him just to hold on
His Pain is so Bad, His Pain is so Bad He Gets Mad
I took the overnight bus ride Just to show him a cared
He has grown a beard Looking like he has done years
Quarters on the table but he wasn't able
To touch the Microwave Or the vending Machine
The Correctional Officer watching us Looking really mean
My nephew smirking and grinning Because he knew he was winning
By me showing my love to my fam Letting them know that he will
Still stand a Man
After we ate I asked him Did he have faith
He was quiet
So, I spoke what I wrote,
Cries of Black
Cries of Black
Cries of Black
Teenage Boys

SOUL'S CONFESSION

Just listen and do not speak
at times, I feel low and very weak
Just this summer four of my Homey's died
I stood over their coffin and could not even cry
They lived in a negative way and said, "This is the only way to survive."
If that were true, they will still be alive
I am not going to front
I have lied, cheated, and stolen too
You will do the same if you know what I go through
It is like I embrace their death'
I know sooner or later I will be next
I am waiting and wondering
When is it my turn
The light of my reality screams in my heart and it burns
A man I am supposed to grow and become
How could that be when my mother never told me where's my father is from?
It is like my mind is clouded with pain
Sometimes I could not think
I am going insane
as soon as I came out of my mother's womb
I have been cursed with my dark black skin, wooly hair and being born first.

ROSEMARY FOLKS

I watch my mother shed tears
as she drinks and tell E&J all her fears
I question asking myself "Can or does God really love me?
How could that be when him I never see?"
He looked at me
With watery eyes
The next thing I knew It was time to say bye
I told him It could be a better way
If you kneel and pray
Cries of Black
Cries of Black
Cries of Black
Teenage Boys.

Don't Worry

I am learning to say to myself
to my inner child
That still exists

>Don't Worry

I am right here
I will hold you
When I remember your lonely cry

>Don't Worry

It wasn't your fault
They violated your soul and spirit
Your person
I will comfort you

>Don't Worry

I too, remember their smell
the taste of their sweat
I have seen your pain
We lived through it

>Don't Worry

ROSEMARY FOLKS

I will take care of you
I tell myself
Don't Worry
I am learning to love all of me
Especially that inner child.
That had no voice That still exists.

Don't Worry.

SOUL'S CONFESSION

Flight 800, Unforgettable lost

Yes, cry and scream out loud
Because you know
You won't see me in physical form again
but after all the anguish is gone
Remember my smile
Never forget that I love you all awhile.

What happened?
Where is the body?
Why me?
At you I am angry God
How could you let this be?
You loved me
Not because of the way I looked
You loved me because
What and how I made you feel
You loved my Spirit Now my Spirit must travel
To our heavenly father above
Think of me When you see God's beautiful white dove.
How am I supposed to go on?
I was used of seeing you I was used to hearing your voice
I did not get a chance to say bye
the last words I heard you say was, "I see you when I get there." It hurts so much knowing you won't be near.

Your love is still alive even in death.

ROSEMARY FOLKS

Homeless Person

"I know you see me, but You refuse to acknowledge my existence   Why is that?"
Are you afraid of becoming like me?
Cause once in your life
You even felt like given up
Without Me
You will never know how strong
You really are

Without me
Your emotional conscious
Would have never traveled far
I would like to say, "Excuse me for the way I smell."
I understand your facial expression
I giggle to myself

When I imagine me asking?
"Can I come with you Home?
I just want to take a quick shower."
You will get so frightened
and ask another for help
Through eye contact.

SOUL'S CONFESSION

Without me
You will never know
how screwed up
This government really is
Some of you
Would not feel a need to give
I still need medication
And more hospitalization
But I have no medical insurance
So, I am forced to live in my head
And having some of you wishing I was dead.

How Can I

    How can I

Say that I
Care for you
When I could not love

    How can I

Give to you my all
When I could not love

    How can I

Lie beside you
When I could not love

    How can I

Show you that
I really do want you
When I could not love

    How could I.

    ? ? ?

I Am Here Not to Raise a Man

I will give you a couple of dollars
Here and there
But when I come home from work
You will kiss me and smell like beer
You said you needed the money to look for work
Who and what do you think I am?
A freaking jerk
Your mama warned me
And your sister did too
I refuse to see all the pain
You put them through
They told me
That in the long run
I will see who you really are
When I tell you
Things are not going right
You will leave and go to the nearest bar
You are old enough
To put a bone
In your back
So, don't try to move your
Belongings in here
When you are not intact

ROSEMARY FOLKS

When you are not intact.
What you see around here
Is what I worked hard for,
And please do not get me wrong
You, I truly adore
And for you
I will do all that I can
But, sweetheart
Let me get one thing straight

                I am here
           Not to raise a Man.

SOUL'S CONFESSION

JAMES BALDWIN

I have been lynching myself
Ever since I have learnt to cry silently
Among shadows in a dark crowded room
I am inhaling burnt flesh
That has never been smelt
I am responding to the burning bush
That spoke to Moses
The hand that writes this is
The helper of many wondering Spirits
That has grieved the hatred that
Surrounds a soul of yesteryears
I am now living in a prophecy
That was spoken of before
I breathed on my own
I am feeling a stabbing in my heart
As I watch
Fathers, Brothers, Nephews, and male Cousins
Give up on life
They blame souls that they could see and touch
So, they loathe
But the real fault belongs to their inabilities to yearn
To Long for an understanding of one's Spirit.

ROSEMARY FOLKS

They have been living their lives in the Present
Saying, they are living in their reality
It distresses me that they do not realize
That the only way to grasp their reality
Is to understand
> **the tears and**
> **struggles of long**
> **ago.**

Melancholy

What is to become of me?
When this life will not be even a memory
I know I need to keep feeding my Soul's appetite
For affection and recognition
By expressing myself through writing, singing
Or reciting the Words that God has entrusting to me
I am tired, but I refuse to lie down
Because the enemy,
Depression is sitting at my bedside
Waiting to comfort me
Waiting to extinguish all my light
That gives me hope
I will not allow myself to be
entangled with this conversant love affair
It is no longer welcomed in my loving arms
I do not accept its romantic antics
The familiarity of its grasp
Is haunting and unpleasant
Once I become one with it
I would be engulfed with the stench of death.

ROSEMARY FOLKS

Music of Miles

Music of Miles
Soothes the inner appetite
For affection
It caresses my emotional wounds
That has been left open by a lover
I connect with feelings
Of loneliness, hurt and pain
As I listen, I give my heart permission to cry
Like his trumpet His wind of life
Gives birth to a sound
That can kill All of life's troubles
A dreamer's reality That is who I am
One would be ignited by their truth
Once they accept all of me
Sound can stimulate a hidden desire
So, can words
What is heard and spoken
Can give life or death
Choosing to kill my need for
Connecting with another
Is like stopping a child's laughter
While it is being tickled, it is painful
Music of Miles
Instructs me to slow it down
All thoughts as well as physical movements
Being still and listening to his gift to the world

SOUL'S CONFESSION

Allows me to unravel my contribution to humankind (writing)
Never hold back and silent what gives life
We were born to create
Give back beauty to the Universe
It was created in love, and for us
Be kind, gentle, loving, peaceable, and understanding toward others

**Relax and listen to the
Music of Miles.**

ROSEMARY FOLKS

Once Again

I am full Once of anger again
and disappointment
I live my life in fantasy of whom I will become
I find it difficult to live in the
Importance of now
I must do what is needed
To live responsibly
There is no one around to take care of me
Financially
I have all what it takes to gain employment
Because today I am employable
If only I do not pick up a drink
Or give into depression
                                                  Once Again.
I cannot afford either of the two
in moments like this
My mind races
Trying to find comfort
in my old way of being
? Signing myself into a psyche ward
                                                  Once Again.

SOUL'S CONFESSION

The desire of not dealing
With my fears, hurt, loneliness, and frustration
Seems welcoming
But that is no longer an option
I will give into this weakness of confusion
By being creative This time around
        I will continue to function
        I will guide my emotions
       Into focusing on my purpose
      of my dreams of performing
                    Once Again.

ROSEMARY FOLKS

Poetry from Within

The sky cries when God enters a soulful Spirit's heart
Whenever the sun's illusion shine on a river bank
Gives me thoughtful wonderment of
Yah's beautiful Earth.
Everything I need to weather the storm is within me
to never know who I am
Would be like an alley cat Rambling in trash for
nourishment.
The sound of traffic jams
the screams of loneliness
A neighbor's furious fist fight and screams
Relaxes me like a jazz piece by Miles Davis.
To withhold love from a loved one
Tells Satan that maybe there is a chance
for his uncanny ways to enter my being
but by sharing my love with loved ones
and even with the ones who hates me
Make My God the Great I AM smile warm heartedly.
Once I have a reason to be unloose
More of me
will be revealed

Prostitute

I am on the street
I am all alone
Where do I go?
Who do I phone?
I ran away from the people
Who were to nurture, protect
and love me
I look up at the sky asking God, "Did you see the touching and groping?"
I wish that someone would have made it stop
But no one had
Now I am on the street hoping to get shot.
I know it is wrong to feel this way
I even wish that I do not make it through another day
I am missing a loving touch
In which a child was supposed to receive
Now here I am A child in a woman's body
Thinking that a man I do not even know
Might find a way to truly love me.

Questionable Farewell

My childhood friend is gone
I did not get a chance to say bye
I have practice every night
On what I will say to her
But now she is gone
Death is something everyone will Come across
The way one chooses to die
Who is it up to?
Does Thy Spirit make the decision on how one should die?
Our lives are like roller coasters
When we are born
We do not know that we are living
We only realize we are alive
Only when we choose to hurt or kill one another.

SOUL'S CONFESSION

Realization

The body of Christ is said to be the church
If you believe just that, you will surely hurt
In this day and time, Christ breathes through Man
But know that the Father, the Son, and the Holy Spirit
Works hand and hand
What is done in the dark will come to the light
Because the light of man will continue to fight
God wants you to depend on him and only him
Turn away from Satan's works
Turn away from gossiping, lying, adultery, fornication and drunkenness
(I too, struggled with the humanist of fleshly desires)
All God wants from his children
Is for us to love one another and to be obedient, and to
REPENT
He loves us, this I know, because his son he has sent
Before you confess your sins openly to another
Make sure that person is a Spiritual sister or brother
Wolves in sheep clothing is the truest statement ever
? sinful spirit will inherit God's Kingdom.
Never

ROSEMARY FOLKS

If you stop listening to the spirit that dwells from within
You will give deceitful beings a chance to begin
To turn your love away from the glory and promise of the true God
You must listen and trust in the Spirit from Above
Once you discern from Truth
from a Lie
That is when you will truly Love.

Response to Cries of Black Teenage Boys

I have kept quiet and let you speak
Now you must listen and know that you are very meek
In the summertime, it is like Satan works overtime
Mentally heating up weak minds
Having them believe that they could get away with any crime
and when Satan is finished with you
He will leave and go on his merry way
That is when you must kneel, confess your sin and pray
You are never alone in your darkness,
the light that shines within you
will guide you and become your compass
Trust that God,
do not look at the outer appearance of persons
He looks from within
Once you believe that, that is when your life will begin
He created you for his own purpose and glory
He wants your life to tell everyone a story

ROSEMARY FOLKS

So, don't get so angry because you do not have
a physical father emotionally around
Know that your Spiritual father will never let you down
A strong black man you will grow and become
Because the heavens are where you are from
When you can feel an inner peace of love for self
No matter what you go through
That is when you will see and feel the presence of God.

SOUL'S CONFESSION

Rooms

Never thought I will need to enter
I thank God, they are around to keep me centered
I walk in not knowing what I will say But I know once I am in I will want to stay
In there I know I need to be Because out here the devil has a hold of me In there I sit and listen to the pain of others
In there I hear the real cries of my sisters and brothers
Never thought I will need to enter I thank God, they exist to keep me centered Most people listen just to judge
But in there some truly understands
And wants to give a hug In there you will hear,
"MY NAME IS____AND I HAVE BEEN DRINKING SINCE I WAS ___ YEAR OLD."
It is in there I realize that God truly saves.
The color of a person is not seen in some rooms
Know that God is colored blind
and that
He is coming soon.

ROSEMARY FOLKS

Silent Rage

I will cover the light
And only I will be seen
My safest haven
Is in my dreams
I will not be moved
I will be only me
In the morning And even at night
For a sight to behold
For I cannot see
My inner being seems guided
By the darkest rainbow
I will show no love
Just a picture to move
My weakness is my strength
My strength is my weakness
To carry all points
To be all groove
The darkest hole Is in my soul And that alone,
Will only moves My tears at night.

Slave Girl

I live because of you
Knowing not that my reality
Was once your dream
I am physically free But mentally and spiritually
I am still in bondage
Your sadness is felt
Your pain is remembered
In my tears
I can hear your voice in my depression
But there is a peacefulness in me
When I can live in Spirit
You are my friend You are my light
I will speak for you
You will not be forgotten
Cause now you live through me.

Solid Foundation

The seed that was planted
Was from a strong spirit
It never needed acceptance
To find its truth
It turned inward to seek wisdom
And it lives by water from above
It's branch of life
Has assisted with many deaths
In which pain staking lynching
Intruded its being
And now their spirit
Lives inside of its bark
When cut in half
you can witness Their life's span
And visually hear the cries of innocence
Belonging to a people That has been stolen.

SOUL'S CONFESSION

Sugar Daddy

There is no one better than
this man my momma called
Daddy
When I was young
He brought me all sorts of toys
He said when I grow up
He would have to fight off all the boys
He brought my momma expensive gifts
Such as diamonds and pearls
He told me
That I was the prettiest little girl
**There is no one better than
this man my momma called Daddy**
He treated me nicer than my brothers and sisters
He even told them to call him Mister
He told me to call him Sugar
Because he said that I was special
At the age of twelve
No one knew I was sexual
**There is no one better than
this man my momma called Daddy**
When I was fifteen
I had a cutest little baby
Momma started drinking
And she asked herself, "Could it be, Maybe?"

ROSEMARY FOLKS

Suicide Reflection and Still I Breathe

I am breathing like a toddler's first steps in life
I am breathing like a fearful run
from a vicious dog barking after me
I am breathing like an asthmatic under attack
I am breathing like I have no reason for life.
My body is feeling all of life's hatred
My body is remembering the violation
My body is drenching in sweat when it is 10 below zero
My body is not connected to the spirit.
Memories of laughter
Memories of Mama's cries
Memories of lies
Memories of hopelessness
Memories of disturbance of words are being felt and heard.
I cry because of many hurtful words hazed my mind
While I am awakening by the voice from within
I journey to the unknown truth
There is no more room for self-pity or self-doubt

SOUL'S CONFESSION

I must keep focus and loosen soul's appetite for stillness
Some stare and shake their heads
Because to them my dreams are dead
to them I have no life
Because my desire in living,
is not to become a wife
I will speak into the world and claim what is mines
Even when it may seem I am being unkind.

ROSEMARY FOLKS

The Devil Never Shines in The Light

The devils can never shine in the light
I know he hates me with all his might
I know it was you who spread those rumours
That is why I have no more sense of humour
When there is no one around, you treat me as if I am down
I made you laugh when you wanted to cry
By me doing my best, you say
I am trying to be "fly"
I never took for granted the times we shared together
You talked about me, in no way did I thought, never
We used to call one another on the phone
Knowing it was you on the other end, I never felt alone
I admitted to you my fears
I was the one always there.
The devil can never shine in the light
I know he hates me with all his might
the old days we sat and reminisced
the whispers, I wonder how I could have missed

SOUL'S CONFESSION

When others talked, you could have walked
But no, instead
Their minds you fed
Saying things about me that was not even true
How could you, when you knew all the pain
I have been through
You do not love me now
and you certainly did not love me then.
The devil can never shine in the light.

ROSEMARY FOLKS

The Last Laugh Is Mines

I know how it feels to be talked about
And laugh at
Behind one's back All my life
It has been like that
I never knew it came from the ones
I have learnt to love
Ask me how I know? He told me
Thy Spirit above.
Someday I will walk in this world
and not care what others say
You know why Cause unlike them
I always pray.
One morning for all the mornings
I will wake up
And walk out with my head Sky-high
They will all stare
And may even be unkind
But I will smile and say to myself
Hmmm, the last laugh is mines.

They Did Not Win

Innocence breathed in hatred
While feelings of confusion and fear
Were forced upon me
Not realizing how strong the stench
Of their aroma
Will envelope my every action
As I am now a woman
Longing tears that have never Falling
Now flows down my cheeks
Like chaotic winds thrashing the sea
I held back so much of self
That I once accepted
I am not lovable
I am now allowing myself to remember
Unwanted touches that haunted me
I am being led toward healing
As I open to her and tell her
My truth
She enlightened me by saying,
"You are doing fine, put words to those tears,
You are perfect just the way you are,
You are where you supposed to be in life."

ROSEMARY FOLKS

I am beginning to believe her words
Could it be her soothing voice
that permits the little girl in me to verbalize her pain?
My creation of dreams is here once again
I am no longer lost
THEY DID NOT WIN
I never knew that this day will come
It was all because of who she was
Her kindness and patience
Encouraged me to write this
She seen me beyond my frustration
She has unwrapped
One of God's precious gifts to this universe

              ME

Thank You Antoinette aka Toni (Therapist)

Voices of The Mind

It's like the mind
Could be unkind
It could make you blind
It could be even deceiving
Having you believing
That everyone who listens has your back
Get caught sleeping
Some fool will attack.
In reality
I question is my mind just fooling me
Lords know I need to be set free
From this way of thinking
Memories of mine past have me sinking
Everything I need to survive is in me
so I give
Some take my kindness for weakness
I know I could beat this
Feeling of hopelessness
So, I use my words as my fist
I am no man trick
I put my trust in the Most High
He is the one that gets me bye
People laugh at me
I know they are laughing at my life
But the last laugh will be mine

ROSEMARY FOLKS

I just needed a little time
To gather my thoughts
Jehovah is the one I fought
Things I should do
I don't
But living for the devil I won't
I am ready to confess my sins
So, my life can begin
I want to live my life full to the end.

SOUL'S CONFESSION

We

Some walk around saying this and that
When they do not know all the facts
God do not like Liars, Gossipers, Whisperers, and Hypocrites
You are which one of this
Why can't we as a people
Find a way to love one another unconditionally
Must we wait for the paradise?
Then that is when it would be finally.
In the spring time
We feel warmth when we see the flowers
Blossom in the grass
Why can't we give one another that when we pass?
At a time in our lives
We will experience having a friend who really cares
When we are down and out
That friend will be there
We should not have to wait to show how precious
Our heart can really shine
It will be too late
When that friend is gone
And their heart is left behind.

When

When I first breathed on my own
You made sure
That I had all ten toes and all ten fingers
When you first heard, me cry
You knew instantly
That I needed you When I first Started to walk
I bet you was so proud When I have first spoken I said,
"Daddy", But you said no Say, "Momma"
When my daddy said to you That I was not his child
When you have screamed,
"someone please save me."
Momma when we were one
I felt your pain
Now that you have given me life I will find a way
for us to survive
I LOVE YOU.

SOUL'S CONFESSION

YOUR THOUGHTS

ROSEMARY FOLKS

SEASON

TWO

SOUL'S CONFESSION

An intimate relationship between lovers is a gift from the Great I Am. It is not just for procreation but truly a gift to Men and Women. Yah loves the bonding of families. He created the Woman for the Man and the Man for the Woman. It is normal to feel an attraction toward the opposite sex and want to have a physical encounter but when abuse and neglect of nurture interrupt the process of maturity, the evil Spirit of Lust overcome one's desires for true Love. I, like so many turned from the appropriate interaction of love to just the physical aspect of Lust. I did not know how to accept Love from the creator of Love. I craved for physical attention which lead to the misuse of my Temple (My Body). I did not have multiples of partners, but I believed that Sex was equivalent to Love. As I read the following poems, I recognized my misunderstanding of genuine acceptable relationships that led to pain, but I also identified the light of hope that still existed in my darkness. I called out to the one who knows me best and who still chooses to Love me unconditionally. Once I accepted Yahushua as my Lord and Savior, I became a wife waiting with eagerness for her husband. Marriage is not just a union with Man and Woman but with Yah and his People. (The True Church.)

ROSEMARY FOLKS

Abrupt Sensuality

My heart is saddening
I have given into fornication
I gave not just only my soul
But a part of my spirit to lust
Now I am so unstable with my inner self
I have asked God to open a door
Of true love and acceptance
But Satan had entered in
I do not know
If Thy Spirit will ever forgive me
But from this day forward
I will say to every open ear
And announce
That he is Mine companion.

SOUL'S CONFESSION

Are You the One

Time will tell My true self will be revealed
I will not mentally project who I think you are
Because my perception of you
Would be who I want you to be
I want to listen to how you feel
I just don't want to explore every inch of your body
I want to connect with you Soulfully, Spiritually, and yes
Physically
When I first saw you
I was not just intrigued with your outer beauty
But with the way you spoke
The sound of your sexy voice
The way you choose word that glides from your lips
I can only image the kind of lover you are
There are so many questions
I want answered
Like, have you ever been in love?
Has anyone broken your heart?
What is your favorited moment?
What do you do to untwine?
What do you do for fun?
Can I spend a day with you?
These questions can go on and on
Allow me to drink your every expression
So, I can be your answered prayer

ROSEMARY FOLKS

I only know you through hear say
And what I hear is not at all true
I will not let other thoughts of you
Hinder what my heart tells me
Sometimes I wonder and ask myself,
"how in the world you continue to smile when the laughter is about you?"
I see glimmer of truth and light when you are around
You bring this feeling of joy to my heart
When I am in your presence
I just want a chance for you to experience love
Like love is supposed to be
Some cannot handle another feeling for them
Like I feel for you
Just by you showing your truth
I know I would enjoy every moment we would share
After you let me in your world
And I let you in mine
We then can build a world of ours.

SOUL'S CONFESSION

But

I will scream
but who will holler
I will close my eyes
but who will see I will turn to you, but you will face the
other way, But I know you will always stay.
I have made you My personal diary
But you have chosen
To put My words against me
I thought you I could trust
When others talked about me
You felt to talk too
As if it was a must.
Why you cannot be who you really are?
Forget what others may say
Believe me
I am in confusion Just like you, But I have knelt and prayed
Asking   God, "Could these
feelings be true?"

ROSEMARY FOLKS

Embracing Thoughts

Thought of you
Always seeps through
My conscious
It is not every day
I think of you
This way
But when I do
I get afraid
Of my own thoughts
I try telling myself
It is wrong
Because of my religious understanding
Without success
I try to stop my thoughts of you
But every time I hear your voice
Every time I think of those late-night phone calls
Every time I notice your stare
Makes it impossible
For me not to think of you
My yearning for you gets stronger
I will embrace these thoughts
I will not wait any longer.
(SIN ACCOMPLISHED)

Emotions Concealed

I feel safe when I am all alone
To share myself with another
Will put me in danger
Anyone can puncture my heart with a sharp object
But to allow my heart
To bleed
For a love like yours
I just could not see myself doing
I can allow myself to love
From the heart
And it would be the purest
Anyone will want to gain
But can anyone say to me,
"My love for you is genuine."

ROSEMARY FOLKS

First Encounter

I see you staring I bet I know
What you are thinking
Her hair is put together
There are no strains out of place
Her outfit fits her
As if she is a run way model
She got to be altogether
I think I will go over
And introduce myself.
Oh, my gosh He is coming my way
Let me act like I am about to yawn
And check mine breathe
I hope the perfume I am wearing
Does not stink He is going to ask me my name
Suppose I forget
Come on legs move
I feel as if I must piss.

God Has Hugged You

When you walk to a place
and you feel safe

                God has hugged you

When you feel at your worst
and somehow you came through,

                God has hugged you

When you have cried a painful cry
When you were alone

                God has hugged you

When someone you have trusted
Have talked about you
and you know this to be true

                God has hugged you

Live in the Word
And focus on what God ask of you
Now it is time for you to hug Yah.

ROSEMARY FOLKS

Hey, Daddy It Is I

In a place where the unknown of self is being raised
I am silent, I am patient
But my inside is trembling
I am afraid
I do not wish to disappoint you
I hear your voice in my chaotic emotions
When others are like a ghost
Their judgment is heard through eye contact
You place me in this Shelter for this season
And I must stay put until I learn the reason
I love you,
Daddy
I love you not because you love me
I love you because coming to you,
is the only way I could be set free
You know my actions before I make a move
You know my heart
A sinner I am
But through my sin
I still wish to worship you
Does that make me a hypocrite?
Does that make you love me any less?
Does that make you turn your ear from my cry?

Hey, Daddy it is I
Your child, Rosemary.

SOUL'S CONFESSION

I Am in Your Hands

Can I feel your love all day long and still live in deceit?
You love me beyond the oceans, rivers, and seas
What a love
What a great love
If I continue to focus on your ways
And live my life for your purpose
All will be well
I am surrendering it all without any assurance
Of what will be next
Oh, father I trust you
For all of life's blessings
For inner clothing
I would never be naked again
Never again will I feel ashamed and confused
You are my best friend
You know my every thought
You know it all.
You know all emotions I feel
You hear what people say and think of me
Does that make you sad?
Did you cry, like I often cried when unkind words were said?

ROSEMARY FOLKS

You teach me to love beyond negative attitudes
Beyond hatred and jealousy
Sometimes I felt weary and did not want to show up for life, but you gently guided me out of my depression, my anger My hurt and lust
You have me longing for your justice, your peace, your patience and your love
What a wonderful God.

SOUL'S CONFESSION

I Still Love You

My time is up
And I lived life because of God's mercy, grace, and love
The breath Thy Spirit have given me
Allowed me to witness the lives of my loved ones
I walked with and talked with God
In soul and in spirit I strayed from Yah
But he opened his loving arms
And welcomed me back
I am comforted;
I am waiting for God's glories Kingdom
To envelop the earth Like it has been envisioned
And know that in that time and hour
I will see you all again
Father, allow your kindness, patience, and understanding
Caress the soul that cries for me because
I am not in physical form
But let them remember my presence via the spirit
I have show

ROSEMARY FOLKS

To the ones who knew me
know that my loving God is watching over you
He hears you when you are asking me for forgiveness
I lived; so, I too, am asking for your forgiveness
We are not Born Saints
But we are Spirit in Soul's body
the quicker you believe that
with not just with your mind
with all of who you are
the happier you will be
the sooner you will be set free.

SOUL'S CONFESSION

I Want to Live

I hear you
I will never shut you out again
You have given me a new way of accepting
All of me
You are my personal diary
You are my friend
You hear what I say
When words are not heard
You tell me to breathe
Yet, I find it difficult at times
You tell me to never to give up
Because my life is worth living
I hear you when you tell me
"Your day will come, who you are supposed to be You will become."
I am finally realizing
Why I react to situations like I do
It is because of the mental and physical trauma
I had in my life
That is why I could numb all emotions
And create turmoil in my life by impulsive decisions
Because of you
Even when I lack faith

ROSEMARY FOLKS

I can focus and get back on track
Thank you for loving me
Thank you for having me love myself
The choices I make in careless moments
hinders my walk and my future
At times, I am unable to feel the light
But when I cry
I have been told
That I am healing
In my serenity, I can hear you say
"Forget what you have heard, it is me you will someday serve."
No matter what I go through
You are there
Holding my hand and guiding me
I will hold my head up high
Because it is your strength
That is being judge
When I am being critiqued
No longer do I want to envision my life in thoughts of fantasy
I WANT TO LIVE.

Inner Talk

Before I was put on this Earth
You knew me
Before I understood how people could be
You knew me
Now I am beginning to imagine
How a part of my Spirit
Is holding onto you for dear life
I need you
If only I could allow my outer being
Shine like my inner being
When I think of you
I will be happy
If only someone will allow their thoughts
To be guided by their heart
And let me in
I will be happy
To finally feel and nurture someone's
Spirit Like mine
My treasures will finally be found.

ROSEMARY FOLKS

Jesus Speak

Be still and let me work through you
Not the other way around
Me being still and you working through me
I need for you to be quiet
I have a perfect plan for you
Thank you for opening your mind and spirit to be used
Recognized it only takes us three
Yahweh (The Father), Yahushua Jesus Christ (Me) and the
Holy Spirit (The Counselor)
To put things in order
You are a part of the loving grace, mercy, and glory of the
Father
No Sweat from your brow will change the course of
Eternity Believe in me, love everyone and Yah with all yours
might Build your faith by coming to the Father in prayer
Allow the Holy Spirit to administer your next move Yes!
You must take actions but be move
by the Spirit of Truth
That rest in you
And not by the negative thoughts of others about you
or your own emotions
You will become who you are supposed to be
I alone died on the Cross for the sin of Man
I am please by your repentance, and your turning away
from sin

SOUL'S CONFESSION

You can no longer carry the burden of others on your shoulder
I need for you to stand upright so that the world could see the workings of our Father
Give me your personal cares
I Got You.
I recognize your reaction to Father's discipline
And I just smile because you are willing to readjust
Your thinking for daddy's
Remember to be used for the Kingdom of Yahweh
You must wait on his timing and not your own
You first must crawl (accept that the words in the Bible as Truth)

Before you walk (Living Holy and Righteously) I LOVE YOU

PS
You are blessed beyond measures.
I am watching over You, and our Father breathes in you. How the world sees You are so far off how me and Daddy sees you. Until we meet face to face.

ROSEMARY FOLKS

Knowingly

My flesh is the thunderstorm
Of my being
If I will allow
People will see and feel my lightening
I can understand why my soul
Is being carried away by lust
Because I have never known love.
As the clock ticks, away
I focus I can hear the seconds (I am fallen into
Lamentation)   A knock on the door
I know who is on the other side
I am afraid to open it because it will be me
Naked
It is true that the mirror has two faces Four desperate eyes
Searching for comfort and compassion
But all in all
It is me in this mirror
What others may picture for me
And what I may feel
Maybe the same
I constantly pray that I will not give into Worldly desires
Because birth to sensual appetite is like sin as

Sin is to death.

SOUL'S CONFESSION

Matthew 6:30, 33

Silent
but I am screaming in anguish
My fundamental needs are not met
Where will I live in the next few hours?
How would I support myself?
I am not weary about what will I eat, drink
Or what I will wear tomorrow
Because I remember the scriptures that says,
Don't worry about what you will put on
or what You will eat or drink
"God clothe the vegetation of the field Which is here today and tomorrow thrown into the fire. Will He not much rather clothe you, you with little faith."
As I move in silence
I remember, "Seek the Kingdom of God above all else, and live righteously, And He will give you everything you need."
My Faith has gotten me through the darkness hours.

ROSEMARY FOLKS

I will praise you Father in my suffering
I will praise you in my anger
I will praise you in my regression
I will praise you in my uncertainty
I will praise you when there is no one around
I will praise you in the biggest of crowds
I will praise you
Not only because you gave your only Begotten Son
Or that you loved me first
It is because I am finally falling in love with you

More of You Less of Me

How could
I be who you want me to be
When I am full of self?
Remove anything that is not of you
I am giving you all of me
That is the only way that I will be free
I am learning to obey your voice
Before I make a choice
Only you can see beyond my circumstances
I am grateful for your love
For this romance
You guide my steps towards right actions
I can now recognize your Spirit's passion
In all decision, I make or have made
Is to bring me closer to you
At the time, I could never see that truth
I always believed it was me who wanted to follow
But with kindness you showed me that Man's thoughts are shallow
You always know what I need, when I need it
YOU ARE IN LOVE WITH ME
I must confess
I have fallen for you as well

ROSEMARY FOLKS

My heart desire is to be intimate with you
Letting you in every area of my life.
From praising you
To revealing all known sins
I appreciate your life
Because in it, I can live
Have your way in me
Show your character through me
When I am in your presence
I am reminded that I belong to Thee.

SOUL'S CONFESSION

My Love

Something in you have me
believing in love once again
you turned my way of thinking upside down
I am ready for you type of loving
I am in this relationship for me
And for once not just for a lover
I want to be here
In your arms Lying on your chest
Hearing what gives your life
I never had anyone show me love Like you
I heard plenty of times
Someone verbally confessing their love for me
but never saying it through actions
I was so afraid of saying with my heart "It is you that I
want and love."
Until I met you
Looking in your eyes
I feel the stimulation of my body's craving
in every inch of my being
Your touch is like no other
My secret desires you hear
Through soundless expressions
Where ever you are
Believe that I am thinking of you
I LOVE YOU.

ROSEMARY FOLKS

Oneness with My Child

In my mother's womb
Without understanding
God carried me in his heart
I have allowed people's laughter and whisper
To separate me from his love
I emotionally and spiritually shut down
I have allowed the pain of love one's loneliness
To surround me in confusion
I shall no longer
The life I breathe now is not my own
I have surrendered to our heavenly father
I have been still and listened to what he had said
He Said,
"I put people in your life, so you will know who you are. I have allowed you to taste forbidden fruit because I knew you will come to me. You are my child. Trust that I have heard what people said about you. I have waited to see how you would respond. I am proud of your response. You have never asked me to hurt them. You have never held any hatred. You came to me and prayed and asked me to forgive them. Asked me to change their hearts. But, know my child that some will never change because some still call my name in vain. Some have come up to you and right before they reached you, whisper to anyone at earshot, "I remember her when.... Or, she still....", and negative words

SOUL'S CONFESSION

sprung forth out of their mouths. But you kept still and obeyed my every word because my love is expressed to mankind through my servants. For you know you will hear the trumpet call, and you will see all evil fall.

My child know that I will never stop carrying you. My child some of their hatred of you will get even stronger. But you keep holding on to your faith a while longer. You are doing what I am asking of you. Even when you feel that you are falling short of my Glory. Continue to tell my Story. Especially when you are being tried and may want to give up and run and hide Stand courageously in my ways until the End of these days."

ROSEMARY FOLKS

Praise

I am truly afraid of change
Because I do not know where I may end up
Deep in my heart I know I will gain
Not just for me but for all
I am happy for the ones I have learned to appreciate,
to care for and love
through them
I am finding out who I am
I thank you Heavenly Father
For allowing me to have faith
And I thank you for giving me this pace.

Realizing

Now I feel I have a reason

To go on

With my hopes and dreams

Even though some of the people I loved is gone

I have finally found a way to cope

I am starting to put my trust in you, Father

Because without you There will be certainly no me.

My Heavenly Father

You know all what I have been through

I truly and honestly thank you

For allowing me to see

what others are thinking

Could this be the reason I am drinking?

Soul's Confession

If I say I will follow I must change
must change
From who I think I am Into who you say I am
I am your child
You saved me For me to be free
From generational sins
Your love has never end
I was so into my wants Not searching for my needs
Not wanting to believe
That we were born to live Not born to die
I must stop the lie.

Me, physically, emotionally, and spiritually loving her
I felt no wrong
I kept hearing Satan's song "Surely you won't die for loving. He gave his only begotten son."
I felt sensual connections
toward the same sex since I can remember.
And felt guilty and ashamed from the start of life
I did not have any desires of becoming a wife
I was okay with just being of service to God's chosen one
Excluding myself from the pack
Because I felt not worthy for such a call
Satan was watching, waiting for me to fall
And I did repeatedly

ROSEMARY FOLKS

But he did not know
when my father will have me be Born Again
He did not know that I will give up all earthly sins
And surrender all fleshly desires
To the Creator of all desires
To the one who saved me from hell's scorching fires
I felt the warmth of the Light that was in my darkness
Reminding me that my life wasn't meant for this
Me accepting the lie of lust
Confusing it with Love
Me accepting the lie of lust Confusing it with Love
I did not want to know the truth from above
But I knew I had to walk through it and carry my cross
Knowing someday I will stand in judgment before the boss
I had to be ready to bury my greatest sin
For my life to begin
It's not going to be comfortable living a new way
But it is possible if I continue to pray.

If I say I will follow you
I must change

1 Corinthians 7:4 "The wife hath not power of her own body, but the husband: and likewise, also the husband hath not power of his own body, but the wife."
GET RIGHT WITH CHRIST

Spirit Is Awake

The spirit is awake I hear the call,
to tell it all His time is up, he is frightened
He is threatened
he is ready for war
The color of a man is not to be judge
It is the heart and spirit of man
There is an authority
That is ready to be uprooted
The liar of false truth
Where would you go?
How do you know?
Who are you?
What will you do?
The time is near
Jehovah, you must fear
Turn from your wicked ways
Stay on your knees and pray
Thy will be done not mines
You must rise and walk in spirit
The revelation is here
Do not go insane
Release all shame
No longer stay in mental pain

ROSEMARY FOLKS

The Silent Whisper

The darkness I have seen
I sat there waiting, not knowing
That the sky will beam
Through the thunder and lightning
I heard you whisper
I even thought that you had said
"Is it you that I shall lift her?"
Please allow me
To make my dreams come true
To make you smile is all I wish to do
A gift you have gave me
Someday it will shape me
Into the child
You wish for me to be
My soul, my Spirit
Will someday be set free.
Your prayers are heard
Speak the Word Of divine love and conquer
No time to doubt
The Spirit is Awake

SOUL'S CONFESSION

Forget your past
Do not repeat your past
Look beyond flesh
And witness in your inner light
Come forth and be healed
It is time for you
To come forth so you can heal others
This world is in need
Welcome the truth
Embrace the truth
Walk in truth
The Spirit is Awake
The Spirit is Awake.

ROSEMARY FOLKS

There Is Only One Way to The Father

Time is running out
Time is running out
Time is running out
He will be here soon.
>**There is only one way to the Father**
>**That is through His son Jesus Christ**

I am tired of them saying
That you are just like all the rest
They could never be you
At their very best
You were born from Spirit and truth
You are immortal
Man, were born from flesh and blood
We are mortal
You were with the Father before the test of time
You knew no sin
But you became sin
So, that Man could be forgiving
Having right standing with the Most High
But Man will continue to strive and try
To be as Holy and Righteous as You
Because, that is what the Father told us to do
We must live in the Spirit and not by the flesh
Better believe we will be given a test

SOUL'S CONFESSION

They keep saying that there is more than one way to get to the Father
It is like they forgot what Jesus said,
John 14:6
"I Am the Way, the Truth, and the Life: no man cometh unto the Father, but by Me."
It is time for us to walk freely.
There is only one way to the Father
That is through His Son Jesus Christ
There is an order in the Kingdom of God
I am not talking about the New World Order
That was created by Satan himself
It is time for you to take down your Bible from the shelf
And get familiar with the works of the devil
He is sly, slick, and having you become a negative rebel
Having you turn your back on the fact
That there is only one way to the Father
And that is through His son Jesus Christ
Rest assure Satan forces will not touch you
Because greater is he who is in you
Than he who is in this world
The truth was in you
Ever since you were a little boy or girl
Repent, turn away from what you know is wrong
The greatest exchanged, your weakness for his strength
So, you could be strong

ROSEMARY FOLKS

Come on now
What are you waiting for?
The End Time is now here
Yes, the God of Israel, Yah, the True God
You must fear.

There is only one way to the Father
That is through His son Jesus Christ

Who side are you on? It is time to decide
You can no longer hide
Because what is done in the dark will come to the light
So, would you please stop putting up a fight?
And just believe and receive God's Salvation, Grace, and Love
From Jesus Christ who is Love
Yah loves all man but hate the sin in man
This you must understand
Some say Satan was never an angel
So please tell me
How did he cross the threshold of Heaven
when only truth and light could only enter?
Pay attention what your mind is centered
Because even the chosen ones would be led astray
That is why we must continue to pray
for thine Truth to be revealed
So, our name could be in the scroll that is still sealed.

There is only one way to the Father
That is through His son Jesus Christ

SOUL'S CONFESSION

The book that gives life, The Bible {Basic Instructions
Before Leaving Earth} Have been tampered with
Some wonder, how could you believe what is in it?
By God exposing Himself to you
And filling you with his Holy Spirit
He gave it to His Son to give to All Believers
Letting us know that he will never leave us
If you believe that Yahushua is the Son of God
And He died for all man's sin
And I believe the same thing too
Why cannot we pray together
And spend time with one another?
Yahweh sees us as all sisters and brothers
> **There is only one way to the Father**
> **That is through His son Jesus Christ**

There is a great energy of deceit in the air
But Yah's Children should never fear
To the throne of Yah, we come Boldly
Yah's fire is in me
The enemy could not own me
So, we believers must go forth fearlessly in speaking the Truth
That is the only reason you would find me in the booth

ROSEMARY FOLKS

1 John 5:4
"For whatsoever is born of Yah overcometh the world: and this is the victory that overcometh the world, even or faith. "
Yah's Kingdom will soon come to this place
There is only one way to the Father
That is through his son Yahushua

SOUL'S CONFESSION

Thinking
to My Heavenly Father

Hearing from you is what I need
Allow me to feel your acceptance
of the choice we have made
To give a voice to the speechless The children
I will put the children first
I will no longer let fear create who I am
No one was there for me
When violations of pain intruded my space
Today I still struggle with intimacy
I still disconnect from self.
Be there for my niece
Have her come to you
Have her rely on your love
Have her feel and acknowledge your presence.
Rape, that demonic generational Curse
Crept into her family in her absence
Infringing on her child's emotions
Finally, that Monster is finally exposed
It would not have her loathe herself
They will require your genuineness
Permit them to soak in your faithfulness
Show me how to be there for her as well as for her children
Because now the child in me finally speaks.

ROSEMARY FOLKS

Thoughts to You

Many have asked "do you have any children?"
I say, "no" They look and question my existence
and wonder why
How can I make them understand?
That the gift you already given me
I must nurture and love it unconditionally
You have given me a powerful way of thinking
And seeing
You govern my every way of life
My actions were leading me quickly into an early death
But now I have turned to you for life's breath
I have asked you for help plenty of times
I have asked you to bring someone into my life
That will love me and have my best interest at heart
I never imagined how me opening my soul to you
That I will realize that the person I was searching for was
me   Your spirit in me makes me see the good in all of
mankind   And by me
not passing judgments
Make people wary of my outer actions
I will talk to the ones who laugh and talked behind my back
I will conquer their hatred of me with the love you freely
give
I know by me focusing on your will for my life
I can stand firmly, and blossom likes my name, Rose

SOUL'S CONFESSION

To you, I owe all that I am
You are the one who help me get through
Sometimes I find myself wondering about your pain
When I see all the injustices in this world
When I hear the sin of gossiping running rapidly amongst your children
And how that sin can change the way people treat one another How it can hinder the brightest person's vision
And how it can turn the light of one's spirit into darkness
"Remember what is said and what is around you, is not who you are."
What others may think of me
Is not what you see nor think
I am trying to live in a way that will make you smile and be proud
It is I who would be lifted into the cloud
Because in the end
It will be your arms
I will rest in.

ROSEMARY FOLKS

Unforeseen Labor

Silent tune of death can be heard
When the history of my family screams out
As I lay, fighting with the soon to be memory of me
to my unborn child
I cry. Normal function for life is to breathe
But I find that act
Too difficult at the present
I can vaguely hear "Come on Push, you can do it, Just one
more time Push."
While my eyes are closed
As I push
and at the same time,
I can see my dead Aunt and deceased Great Grandmother
smiling and encouraging me to take their hands moisture of
pain rolls down my left cheek
as I peek and stare at the powder blue wall
a physical being is gazing at me saying,
"Breathe, it is not your time."

SOUL'S CONFESSION

You Are in Me

I cannot deny my longing for you
When my heart desires are shown through my tears
I tremble just imagining you holding me
If given a chance, to rest on your chest
I know my soul will crumble into millions of pieces
To wake up in your arms
I will breathe new air
My mornings will be full of sunshine
My nights full of joy
Knowing that my life is guided by your acceptance
I will unravel all hope
I will give vision to the blind
Give voice to the mute
And give sound to the deaf.
I will be the garden of everlasting love
Because you are in me.

ROSEMARY FOLKS

You See Me with Your Heart

A relationship is full of moments
Some good some bad
came to me when I was going through Emotions
I could not see you at first
I was to consume with what I thought I needed
I wanted someone who had stability which me, myself
Did not possess
You see exactly who I am And still you want me
You accept things about me in which
I have not accepted myself
I sometimes I ask myself
"What did I do to deserve someone who is so loving,
patient, understanding and compassionate?"
Sometimes I feel I neglect you But I get reassured
When out of nowhere
You enter my thoughts and I replay the last time
You have allowed me to please you
Without asking much of me
And that makes me want to give you my all
In crowds of people I sometimes get nerves
And when we are at parties
You realize my uneasiness
And make up an excuse and get or belongings
And we leave It is moments like that
When I realize how blessed I am

SOUL'S CONFESSION

You have chosen me to love unconditionally
And I thank you Most of the time when we fight
It is because of my own insecurities I am now able to see that
Because of whom you are
When one of us needs space
We can give it
Because we just don't lie together
We also pray together
We also put God first
You taught me how to go to him
When I think, no one understands
You know that there are certain things
I could Only get from him
I used to think when people say,
"I have finally found my soul"
They were full of it But now I know what they mean
You are not just my Soul mate
You are my Spirit mate You make me feel
I can do anything I dream
You make me realize that
Life is for loving
If I am unable to receive love I know for sure
I will be incapable of giving love
I have learnt so much from you
I could only pray that I am giving you
All that you are giving me With you, love is deeply felt.

ROSEMARY FOLKS

Your Groove Moves Me

Can't remember the last time
I was in an intimate groove
Whereas I am all alone I envision you
The phone will ring, I'll pick up
And it's your voice on the other end of the receiver
Just hearing your thoughts Makes me shiver
I sometimes wonder if I can deliver The type of love You
privately hunger for
I want to give you more In a crowded room
When all eyes are on me
It's only your gaze That captivates my heart
You speak so encouragingly when I tell you of my dreams
Being in your presence I feel like a tenor sax
Being played so smoothly, teasingly
And oh, so gently
I invite you to explore my every essence
Your groove caresses me
Like the feeling of a soft cool breeze
On my caramel skin
On a scorching summer day
Don't know when this enticing emotion
Will ever ends But when it does
Promise me we will always remain friends
You have allowed me

SOUL'S CONFESSION

To dig within
To enjoy my every desire
And only you baby
Can singe this inner fire
I finally met someone who is not
Threatened by my knowledge
Of my self-worth
With you, I am not ashamed to admit
When I need help Just thinking of you
I become mesmerized
With your style of grace
And with you I have finally found my place
Because
Your groove moves me.

ROSEMARY FOLKS

Words created the Universe and these words that came from Soul's Heart were created by my life's experiences. As I created this book, I was reminded how my disconnection from the true essence of self hindered my Spiritual journey. My relationship with Yahushua (Jesus) has helped me to look beyond my circumstances to find a hope and a peace. There is nothing that Man can do that could separate us from the Love of the Great I AM. He has given us a free will to live here on this Earth. The choices that we make and what we believe as individuals will determine how we will live in this world. I now have an intimate relationship with Yah through his Son Yahushua (Jesus). I am no longer afraid to share my gifts; which is the ability to articulate my emotions through written expression. The character of Man is evident through one's behaviors and desires. I was engulfed with darkness. I was depressed, a drunkard, and I was living immorally. These behaviors led me to become homeless. I did not live on the street or on Subways, but I lived on family's sofas, on a friend's floor, in rented rooms, at a City Shelter, at a "Christian" shelter, and at a SRO (single room occupancy). I believe that all true Children of the Great I AM, (True Followers of Yahushua) are homeless because this world is not our home.

SOUL'S CONFESSION

This book of authentic suffering was created to remind me that apart from Yahushua (Jesus), I would have stayed in a state of confusion. I pray that this book ignited a burning desire in you to establish a relationship with our Lord and Savior Yahushua (Jesus) so that you will know the True God of all Creation, the Great I AM. Experience unconditional Love so you could live in total Victory.

I welcome any comments and/or feedback about this book. Email me at spiritlivesnu@gmail.com Yah Bless.

ROSEMARY FOLKS
YOUR THOUGHTS

www.ingramcontent.com/pod-product-compliance
Lightning Source LLC
LaVergne TN
LVHW011210080426
835508LV00007B/703